FRIENDSHIP AND FREEDOM

A Play About Addy

ADDY ✹ 1864

DIRECTOR'S GUIDE

THE AMERICAN GIRLS COLLECTION®

CONTENTS

First Edition.
Printed in the United States of America.
94 95 96 97 98 99 WCR 10 9 8 7 6 5 4 3 2 1

The American Girls Collection® and Addy Walker™
are trademarks of Pleasant Company Incorporated.

PICTURE CREDITS
The following organizations have generously given
permission to reprint illustrations:
Pages 3, 13—Harvard Theatre Collection; 7—Bayside Plantation Records,
Southern Historical Collection, University of North Carolina, Chapel Hill (banjos);
11—*Harper's Weekly* (top); 11—Bettmann Archive (bottom).

SPECIAL THANKS TO
Alison Babusci
Gregory Brumfield
Sam Leaton Sebesta
Lynda Sharpe and her daughter Jennifer Sharpe

NOTE: *Friendship and Freedom* may be performed without royalty payments by young people
at home and school and by nonprofit organizations, provided that no admission is charged. All
other rights, including professional, amateur (other than described above), motion picture,
recitation, lecturing, performance, public reading, radio broadcasting, and television performing rights, are strictly reserved. Inquiries about rights should be addressed to: Book Editor,
Pleasant Company Publications Incorporated, 8400 Fairway Place, P.O. Box 620998, Middleton,
WI 53562.

Play Adapted by Valerie Tripp from *Addy Learns a Lesson*, by Connie Porter.

Director's Guide Written by Harriet Brown and Tamara England
Edited by Tamara England and Roberta Johnson
Art Directed and Designed by Craig Smith and Jane S. Varda
Playbill Designed by Kathleen A. Brown
Produced by Karen Bennett, Laura Paulini, and Pat Tuchscherer
Cover Illustration by Susan Mahal
Inside Illustrations by Dan Andreasen, Geri Strigenz Bourget, Renée Graef,
George Sebok, and Jane S. Varda
Historical and Picture Research by Rebecca Sample Bernstein,
Tamara England, Patti Sinclair, and Doreen Smith

Library of Congress Cataloging-in-Publication Data
Tripp, Valerie, 1951–
Addy's theater kit : a play about Addy for you and your friends to perform. — 1st ed.
p. cm. — (The American girls collection. American girls pastimes)
"Addy 1864"—
"Play adapted by Valerie Tripp from Addy learns a lesson, by Connie Porter"—Verso t.p.
Summary: After escaping from a plantation in North Carolina, Addy and her mother arrive
in Philadelphia, where Addy goes to school and learns a lesson in true friendship.
ISBN 1-56247-125-2 (pbk.)
1. Children's plays—Presentation, etc. 2. Theater—Production and direction.
3. Children's plays, American. [1. Fugitive slaves—Drama.
2. Afro-Americans—Drama. 3. Friendship—Drama. 4. Schools—Drama. 5. United States—
History—Civil War, 1861–1865—Drama. 6. Plays.]
I. Porter, Connie Rose, 1959– Addy learns a lesson. II. Title. III. Series.
PN3157.T744   1994   792.9'2—dc20   94–28339   CIP   AC

INTRODUCTION

Addy Walker was nine years old when she and her mother made a dangerous escape from slavery in the midst of the Civil War. Addy and her mother settled in Philadelphia, where they could live in freedom. Addy could finally go to school. But even in freedom, life was hard for many African Americans in 1864. Like the Walkers, many families were separated by slavery and by the war. In Philadelphia, Addy and her mother worked hard and never gave up hope that their family would be reunited. *Friendship and Freedom* tells the story of Addy's hard work in school and of the important lessons she learned there.

Planning and acting out a play is a fun way for you and your friends to spend an afternoon or a day. But Addy did not have much time for entertainment when she was growing up. Many black children worked hard when they weren't in school, helping their parents earn money so their families could survive. Children like Addy might have seen puppet shows or shadow plays at church, but they probably did not get to see plays in theaters. One of the most popular plays during the Civil War was *Uncle Tom's Cabin*, a play about the evils of slavery.

Learning about Addy's new life in freedom will help you imagine what it was like to grow up in Addy's time. Performing the play for your friends and family will help bring history alive for you and your audience today.

ADDY ☀ 1864

Addy's story is one shared by many African Americans who lived during Addy's time. The courage they needed to survive and escape from slavery helped them face the choices and challenges of freedom.

Ira Aldridge, one of the first African-American actors, left America in 1825 to act in England, where he faced less prejudice.

PLANNING THE PLAY

PLANNING THE PLAY

1. *Choose roles and jobs.*

2. *Decide what kind of production you'll have: With or without costumes? Lines memorized or not?*

3. *Plan the action and rehearse.*

4. *Make or find sets, props, and costumes.*

5. *Make a playbill, programs, and tickets.*

6. *Have a dress rehearsal, if you'd like.*

7. *Perform the play!*

PLAY SUMMARY

The play takes place in the fall of 1864. Addy Walker and her mother have escaped from slavery and settled in Philadelphia. As the play begins, Addy is about to start school. So far, freedom has not been what she expected. She and her mother live in a cold, dark *garret*, or attic. Her mother works long hours as a seamstress and Addy hardly ever gets to see her. Worst of all, they still don't know where Addy's father and brother are. Going to school for the very first time is exciting, but Addy learns more in school than just reading and writing. She learns about friendship and freedom as well.

PARTS TO PLAY AND JOBS TO DO

There are six characters in Addy's play, but as few as four actors can put on the play if some people take more than one part. The four **Play Scripts** in this kit include all the parts, and actors can share script books.

But it takes more than just actors to put on a play! Invite other friends to help as *stagehands* or *ushers*. Stagehands create sets and props and move scenery around during the performance, and ushers take tickets and lead the audience to their seats.

This **Director's Guide** gives you ideas for planning and putting on the play. It will help you and your friends decide which parts to play, who will do what jobs, and how to get the jobs done.

Ushers can tear the tickets when they collect them.

STAGING THE PLAY

You can make your production of *Friendship and Freedom* as simple or as elaborate as you'd like. You can decide if actors should read their lines or memorize them. You can act out the play on a real stage or in a living room. The sets can be plain or fancy. You can perform for an audience or just for yourselves, with no audience. Look for ideas about stage sets, costumes, and props in the other sections of this book.

PLAYBILL AND PROGRAMS

Use the playbill poster in the back of this book to advertise your play. You can also make programs and tickets like those on page 15. Playbills and programs tell the names of the actors and the parts acted by everyone in the play. They list the director's name and the names of all the people who helped with costumes, props, and scenery. Ushers can give out programs as they take tickets and lead the audience to their seats.

BREAK A LEG!

Keep the playbill and a copy of your program to help you remember your performance of *Friendship and Freedom*. Many actors keep a *play box* in which they store props and costumes. You can start your own play box and add to it each time you are in a play, just as professional actors do.

It's bad luck to say "Good luck" to anyone going onstage. Instead, say "Break a leg." And at the end of the show, don't forget the curtain call! It's your chance to bow and curtsy while the audience claps.

LENGTH OF THE PLAY

*Friendship and Freedom can be performed in about 20 minutes. You can also have a 10-minute **intermission**, or break, between Act Two and Act Three.*

Uncle Tom's Cabin, advertised in this playbill, was such a popular play during the Civil War that some cities had several theaters playing it at the same time! Cordelia Howard, who became famous for her role as Little Eva in this play, is shown on page 13.

THE CHARACTERS

HOW TO BECOME YOUR CHARACTER

☀ *Close your eyes and imagine that you are your character. Then practice walking, talking, and moving as you think your character would.*

☀ *Your imagination is your best tool for a successful performance. If you don't have a stage or elaborate props and costumes, act as if you do!*

There are six characters in Addy's play. But you can put on the play with just four people if one actor takes the parts of Momma and Harriet and another actor takes the parts of Miss Dunn and Mavis. If you have more than six actors, the "extras" can play students in the classroom scenes.

Don't worry about finding actors who look exactly like the pictures of the characters. Good acting will turn actors into believable characters no matter what they look like!

ADDY is nine years old. She is bright, loving, and hopeful. She has faced the many changes in her life with courage. Now she must find the courage to deal with the choices and challenges that freedom brings.

SARAH is a nine-year-old girl who is Addy's best friend. She walks tall, with an honest pride in herself. She has a wide, warm smile and a face that shows her feelings. She believes in speaking her mind, but she is a loyal friend.

MOMMA is Addy's mother. She works hard as a seamstress and hopes that her family will be reunited soon in Philadelphia. She is a strong, calm woman who can comfort her daughter with a hug and a word.

ADDY

SARAH

MOMMA

MISS DUNN is Addy's teacher. She is warm and kind to her students, but when she has something important to say, her firm voice rings out strongly through the classroom. She stands straight and tall, with excellent posture.

MISS DUNN

HARRIET is a wealthy, snobby nine-year-old classmate of Addy's. She speaks loudly and flounces when she walks to draw attention to herself and to show what she thinks of everyone else.

MAVIS is Harriet's friend and is also nine years old. Like Harriet, she is mean to the other girls.

OTHER JOBS

There are many behind-the-scenes jobs in every play. Decide with your friends who will play which character, who will be the director, who will make costumes, props, and sets, and who will be in charge of music and lights. Actors can also help out as stagehands.

HARRIET

MAVIS

Stagehands who move scenery will be less noticeable if they wear dark pants and shirts. But if they dress up as students from Miss Dunn's class, they will be able to join the performance as extras during some of the scenes.

If actors memorize their lines, you may need a *prompter*. The prompter follows the play in a script book and whispers lines from offstage if an actor forgets them.

At the end of your performance, make sure that everyone who helped put on the show takes a bow at the curtain call!

IF YOU FORGET YOUR LINES . . .

☀ *If you forget your lines and can't hear the prompter, just think about what your character would say and then **ad lib** (say it in your own words).*

THE DIRECTOR

P lays are exciting because lots of people work together to make them happen. But it's usually helpful to have one person be the director. The director is the person who is in charge of the play. That doesn't mean that she is the boss. The director needs to listen to other people's ideas about what should happen onstage. The more the director listens to everyone's ideas, the better the play will be.

GETTING INTO CHARACTER

One of your most important jobs as the director is to help an actor "get into character" by helping her

Addy is happy to discover that her new teacher is so kind and understanding.

imagine what it would be like to truly be that character. What words describe the character? How would the character show happiness or anger? For example, would she smile shyly or laugh out loud when she is pleased? Would she stamp her foot in anger?

You can also encourage the actor to practice walking and talking as the character would. How would Addy walk? How would her voice change when she is excited or sad? Asking these kinds of questions and helping the actors find answers will create a more believable performance.

BLOCKING THE ACTION

As the director, you help the actors plan how to move onstage. This is called *blocking the action*. Blocking usually takes place during rehearsal. The Play Script sometimes tells the actors how and when to move, but it is your job to give additional directions. You also give the actors little signs, or *cues*, about when to go onstage and offstage.

When you are blocking the action, try to use every part of the stage. Important action should take place near the front of the stage, close to the audience.

Actors should face the audience most of the time when they're speaking so the audience can see the actors' faces and hear their lines. But sometimes you might ask an actor to turn away to show that her character is upset or sad. For example, Sarah might turn away to fight back tears when Addy decides to walk home with Harriet and Mavis in Act Four.

KEEPING THE PLAY MOVING

Keep the play moving by helping the actors *overlap* their lines. To overlap, an actor says her first word just as the actor before says her last word. Combine overlapping with occasional pauses to make the play more lively and natural.

PRAISING THE ACTORS

One of your most important roles as director is to praise the actors. Watch for good things that happen during rehearsals and make them part of the finished performance. The best praise is specific and sincere. Many directors keep a notebook handy so they can make notes about things to remember and praise.

MUSIC AND MOOD

Before the show and during scene changes and intermission, set the mood with music. Songs of the Civil War era or spirituals such as "This Little Light of Mine" or "Swing Low, Sweet Chariot" will create the mood of Addy's world in 1864. The librarian in your school or public library should be able to help you find the right music.

Just before the play starts, the stagehand in charge of music can **fade out** *the music by slowly lowering the volume until it can no longer be heard.*

THE STAGE

I t'll be easier to talk about how to move during the play if everyone knows how the stage is laid out. There are special terms to describe the front, back, and sides of the stage. These terms are used all around the world today, from New York to London. They are the terms that actors in Addy's time used, too.

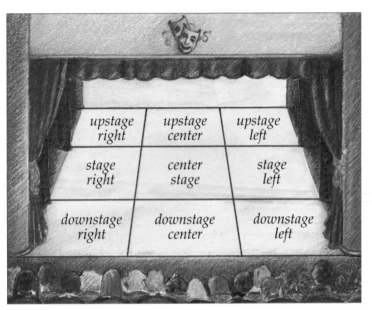

Stages used to be built on a slant, with the back part of the stage higher than the front. This angle allowed the audience to see the actors better. The terms *upstage* and *downstage* come from the way the stage slanted. *Upstage* is the area farthest from the audience—the area that used to be higher. *Downstage* is the front of the stage, nearest the audience. An actor standing in the exact middle of the stage is at *center stage*.

When an actor stands at center stage, facing the audience, the area to the actor's right is *stage right* and the area to the actor's left is *stage left*. The best way to remember *stage right* and *stage left* is to face the audience.

In a good production, you use every part of the stage. The action moves around. When you block the action in *Friendship and Freedom*, try to use these terms so everyone will know exactly where to move onstage.

PROPS

Props can be simple or elaborate, real or made-up. Sets can be dressed up with realistic, detailed props or with simple items that just resemble the real things. Or actors can just pretend they are holding props and let the audience use its imagination!

Here are some ideas for making or finding the props in this play. Be sure to ask an adult before you use things from your home.

Use small tin pails, if you have them, for the lunch pails. Small plastic pails—the kind used for playing on the beach—can also be used. You can easily cover them with tinfoil to make them look more like metal. Tie a scrap of brightly-colored fabric to the handle. Scraps like this helped children identify their lunch pails.

The slates can be small chalkboards, and you can use pieces of chalk for the slate pencils. To make the packages of clothes, wrap clothing, old sheets, or crumpled newspapers in brown paper and tie string around them. Use a marker to write a name and address on each package.

The medal could be a pretty pin borrowed from your mother (with her permission!). You could also make a medal like one described on page 14. The L-O-V-E cookies can be real cookies baked in the shapes of those letters or they can be cut out of felt or cloth. You could also make the letters out of clay.

PROPS

☀

ACT ONE
Two lunch pails
Hair ribbons

•

ACT TWO
A slate
A slate pencil

•

ACT THREE
Two lunch pails
A bunch of grapes
Schoolbooks
Packages of clothes
A handkerchief

•

ACT FOUR
Four lunch pails
Schoolbooks
An apple

•

ACT FIVE
A medal
A lunch pail
L-O-V-E cookies

STAGE SETS

SCENES

ACT ONE
Early morning in the garret where Addy and Momma live

•

ACT TWO
At school

•

ACT THREE
Outside Mrs. Ford's dress shop, after school

•

ACT FOUR
Outside Mrs. Ford's dress shop, after school

•

ACT FIVE
At school

Your sets can be as simple or as elaborate as you want. *Friendship and Freedom* has three indoor scenes and two outdoor scenes, and you will need three sets. You can use the same basic set, but change the way it looks between acts.

One way to create a background is by using large paper to make a mural. Light-brown paper across the back of your stage works best. You can make cutouts to pin or lightly tape to the mural so you can change them from scene to scene. Use paint or chalk to add details on the cutouts and the mural. Applying paint with a large sponge is fast and adds texture.

A simple table, two chairs, and a folding cot can set the scene in the garret.

Push pairs of chairs together in rows to make the classroom with its double desks. Put a chair and small table at the front for the teacher. A cutout or painted-on blackboard at the front of the room gives it the feeling of a school, and so do books and a globe sitting on the teacher's table or desk.

The door of the dress shop could be a real opening, cut into the background. Or it could be painted on one edge of the background, so that the actors can come around the side of the background as if they were coming through a real door.

In the garret.

At school.

Outside Mrs. Ford's dress shop.

CURTAINS

If you don't have a curtain that you can close between acts, actors can simply finish what they are saying and exit at the end of the act. Stagehands can quietly set the stage for the next act. You could also have a *blackout* by having a stagehand turn off the lights just before the actors leave the stage and then turn them back on when the stage is reset. When you are ready to start the next act, place a sign that says "At School" or "Outside Mrs. Ford's Dress Shop" on an easel or chair to tell the audience where the new act takes place. Or a stagehand can hold the sign. Signs can also tell how much time has passed.

THEATER FIRES

In the 1860s, theaters were lit by **gaslights.** *Gaslights created a bright, steady flame because they were fueled by gas—but they were also quite dangerous. The ballet dancer in the lower left corner of this illustration has gotten too close to the gaslights, and her costume is on fire. Before electric lighting, many actors were hurt in this way, and many theaters burned down.*

LIGHTING

Use lights to set the mood. It is a little dark inside the garret in Act One. The classroom in Acts Two and Five should be brighter. Acts Three and Four take place outside in bright afternoon light.

LINCOLN AT THE FORD THEATER

On April 14, 1865, five days after the Civil War ended, President Abraham Lincoln went to a play at the Ford Theater in Washington, D.C. He was sitting in the presidential box when an actor named John Wilkes Booth shot him. Lincoln died the next day. Booth escaped, but was later caught and killed himself.

COSTUMES

COSTUME TIPS

☀ The very simplest way to identify characters doesn't even require costumes! An actor can wear a sign around her neck with her character's name printed on it. This way, actors can easily switch parts without having to switch costumes!

☀ A long-sleeved white shirt with the sleeves tied around the waist makes a fine half-apron for Momma.

Costumes help bring a play to life. They also help the audience identify the characters. Your costumes can be as simple or fancy as you want.

For an elaborate production, you could rent or borrow costumes of the 1860s from a costume shop. Or you could make your own costumes.

But you don't need historical costumes to make your characters come to life. Actors can perform without costumes, or you can create costumes out of simple things in your own closet or your family's closets. Be sure to ask for permission first! And remember, the actors don't have to look like the characters to be believable. If they imagine themselves as the characters and act that way, they'll convince the audience no matter what they look like or what they're wearing.

ADDY wears a long-sleeved white blouse with a bow and a calf-length skirt and matching jacket. She wears dark stockings, and black ankle boots. Her hair is braided back from her face and tied with a ribbon that matches her skirt and jacket. She wears small hoop earrings.

SARAH wears a long-sleeved, calf-length dress, dark stockings, and dark ankle boots. Her dress is plainer than Addy's. Her hair is cut short and she wears the same style of earrings as Addy.

MOMMA wears a simple long-sleeved, ankle-length dress, dark stockings, and dark ankle boots. Her hair is pulled back into a low bun and she wears small hoop earrings. She may also wear a tape measure around her neck and an apron.

MISS DUNN's clothes are the same style as Momma's, but they are nicer, with lace around the collar or bodice. She may wear a shawl. Her hair is pulled back into a low bun and held in place with a *snood*, or small net. She wears earrings and may wear glasses.

HARRIET wears a fancy long-sleeved, calf-length dress with a full skirt, dark stockings, and dark ankle boots. Her hair is long and loose, and she wears a puffy bow that matches her dress. She also wears earrings.

MAVIS's clothes are the same style as Harriet's, but a little less fancy. She wears earrings and a simple ribbon in her hair.

QUICK CHANGES

☀ *Practice making quick costume changes. The actor who plays Momma and Harriet can remove Momma's apron and tape measure at the end of Act One and add a full petticoat under her skirt to play Harriet. She can also let her hair go loose and add a fancy hair bow.*

☀ *The actor who plays Miss Dunn and Mavis changes costumes twice. She should remove Miss Dunn's glasses and shawl and exchange her snood for a hair ribbon when she plays Mavis.*

CORDELIA HOWARD

*In the 1850s and 1860s, the actor Cordelia Howard was popular with American audiences as Little Eva, a character in the play **Uncle Tom's Cabin.** Cordelia's parents were actors, too, and she traveled from town to town with them to perform. She was just four years old when she started acting onstage!*

MAKING A MEDAL

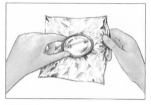

PIN-ON BUTTON
Be careful not to poke yourself as you wrap the button!

REGULAR BUTTON
Use a small loop of tape to attach this medal to Addy's jacket.

Here are two easy ways you can make a medal like the one Addy wins in the spelling match.

USING A PIN-ON BUTTON

First, find a pin-on button—the kind that has a slogan or a funny saying—that is about 1 to 1½ inches in diameter. Cover the button with tinfoil so that the face of the medal is smooth and shiny. To make the medal look fancier, tape or glue a piece of blue or red ribbon to the bottom of the button. Use a ribbon that's a different color from Addy's outfit. The ribbon should be about the same width as the button. Trim the bottom of the ribbon into a "V" shape, as shown. The button can be pinned on Addy's jacket by Miss Dunn in the last act of the play.

USING A REGULAR BUTTON

Begin with a regular button that is 1 to 1½ inches wide. Cover it with tinfoil so that the front is smooth and shiny. Then cut a small piece of poster board or lightweight cardboard so that it is about 2 inches across and ½ inch high. Cut the corners so that they are slightly rounded. Cover the poster board with a small piece of tinfoil and make it a little wrinkled to give it texture. Then attach the button to the foil strip with a piece of clear tape across the back of the button and the strip. You can color the wrinkled tinfoil with a yellow marker to make it look gold.

Put a small loop of masking tape or adhesive tape on the back of the poster board piece so that Miss Dunn can attach the medal to Addy's jacket.

Program

FRIENDSHIP AND FREEDOM

A play in five acts about Addy Walker, a nine-year-old girl who escaped from slavery during the Civil War and made a new life for herself in freedom. The play starts as Addy gets ready for her first day of school in Philadelphia.

Starring   _____ *as Addy*

                        _____ *as Sarah*

                        _____ *as Momma*

                        _____ *as Miss Dunn*

                        _____ *as Harriet*

                        _____ *as Mavis*

Director   _____

Stagehands   _____

_____

Date _____ *Time* _____

Place _____

*You may photocopy or make a ticket and program like these for your performance of **Friendship and Freedom**.*

There are Theater Kits for all five characters in The American Girls Collection. Each kit has a play for you and your friends to perform:

Tea for Felicity lets you act out Felicity's life in the colonies. Felicity learns about friendship and loyalty while America teeters on the brink of the Revolutionary War.

The play *Home Is Where the Heart Is* tells the story of Kirsten's long journey from Sweden to a new home on America's frontier.

In *Friendship and Freedom,* Addy goes to school for the first time and learns to read. She learns about the challenges and joys of being a true friend, too.

The play *Actions Speak Louder Than Words* brings Samantha's world to life. She meets Nellie—a poor girl who works next door—and gives up her greatest treasure.

War on the Home Front is a play about Molly and her friends during World War Two. They nearly start another war when they try to get back at Molly's brother.

Putting on these plays will help you imagine what it was like to grow up in times past and will bring history alive for you and your audience today!

AMERICAN GIRLS PASTIMES™
Activities from the Past for Girls of Today

You'll enjoy all the Pastimes books about your favorite characters in The American Girls Collection®.

Learn to cook foods that Felicity, Kirsten, Addy, Samantha, and Molly loved with the Pastimes **COOKBOOKS.** They're filled with great recipes and fun party ideas.

Make the same crafts that your favorite American Girls character made. Each of the **CRAFT BOOKS** has simple step-by-step instructions and fascinating historical facts.

Imagine that you are your favorite American Girls character as you stage a play about her. Each of the **THEATER KITS** has four Play Scripts and a Director's Guide.

Learn about fashions of the past as you cut out the ten outfits in each of the **PAPER DOLL KITS.** Each kit also contains a make-it-yourself book plus historical fun facts.

There are **CRAFT KITS** for each character with directions and supplies to make 3 crafts from the Pastimes Craft Books. Craft Kits are available only through Pleasant Company's catalogue, which you can request by filling out the postcard below.

Turn the page to learn more about the other delights in The American Girls Collection. ⟶

I'm an American girl who loves to get mail. Please send me a catalogue of The American Girls Collection®:

My name is_____

My address is_____

City_____   State _____   Zip _____

Parent's signature_____

1961

And send a catalogue to my friend:

My friend's name is_____

Address_____

City_____   State _____   Zip _____

1225

THE AMERICAN GIRLS COLLECTION®

The American Girls Collection tells the stories of five lively nine-year-old girls who lived long ago—Felicity, Kirsten, Addy, Samantha, and Molly. You can read about their adventures in a series of beautifully illustrated books of historical fiction. By reading these books, you'll learn what growing up was like in times past.

There is also a lovable doll for each character with beautiful clothes and lots of wonderful accessories. The dolls and their accessories make the stories of the past come alive today for American girls like you.

The American Girls Collection is for you if you love to curl up with a good book. It's for you if you like to play with dolls and act out stories. It's for you if you want something so special that you will treasure it for years to come.

To learn more about The American Girls Collection, fill out the postcard on the other side of the page and mail it to Pleasant Company, or call **1-800-845-0005.** We will send you a free catalogue about all the books, dolls, dresses, and other delights in The American Girls Collection.

FRIENDSHIP AND FREEDOM

✸

A Play About Addy

ADDY ✸ 1864

PLAY SCRIPT

THE AMERICAN GIRLS COLLECTION®

Published by Pleasant Company Publications Incorporated
© Copyright 1994 by Pleasant Company Incorporated
For information, address: Book Editor,
Pleasant Company Publications Incorporated,
8400 Fairway Place, P.O. Box 620998, Middleton, WI 53562.

First Edition.
Printed in the United States of America.
94 95 96 97 98 99 WCR 10 9 8 7 6 5 4 3 2 1

Play adapted by Valerie Tripp from *Addy Learns a Lesson,* by Connie Porter.

Edited by Tamara England
Designed and Art Directed by Craig Smith

ISBN 1-56247-125-2

FRIENDSHIP AND FREEDOM
A Play About Addy

CHARACTERS

ADDY

A nine-year-old girl who has escaped from slavery with her mother and has a new life in freedom

MOMMA

Addy's mother, who works hard as a seamstress and hopes her family will be reunited in freedom

SARAH

Addy's best friend, who is also nine years old and who is helping Addy learn about life in Philadelphia

MISS DUNN

Addy's kind and helpful teacher

HARRIET

A rich and snobby nine-year-old girl at Addy's school

MAVIS

Harriet's friend, who is also nine years old

The action takes place in the fall of 1864, in Philadelphia.

ACT ONE

Scene: The small garret where Addy and her mother live, above the dress shop where Momma works. Momma is standing behind Addy, braiding Addy's hair.

MOMMA: Your Poppa'd be proud to see you going off to the first day of school.

ADDY: *(sadly)* I wish we knew where Poppa and Sam are. I miss them and Esther so much.

MOMMA: I do, too. It broke my heart to leave Esther behind. But we couldn't bring her with us. We never would've gotten away from the plantation like we did.

ADDY: They won't sell her like they sold Poppa and Sam, will they?

MOMMA: No, Addy. She's just a baby. And at least we know Esther's safe.

ADDY: When we gonna live together again like a real family?

MOMMA: I don't know, Addy. *(firmly)* But I do know we still a family, even though we ain't all in one place.

ADDY: I wish you didn't have to work so hard. *(pauses)* This ain't the way I dreamed freedom would be. We got to buy everything now—food, candles, coal, matches. And it all cost so much.

MOMMA: Freedom got a cost. It cost money and hard work and heartache. But there ain't nobody here that own us, and beat us, and work us like animals. I got me a paying job. And you can go to school and learn to read and write. *(Momma finishes tying a ribbon on Addy's braids.)*

ADDY: I'm gonna work hard at school, Momma.

MOMMA: *(hugging Addy)* I know you will. You a smart girl.

(Sarah ENTERS, carrying a lunch pail.)

SARAH: *(excited)* You ready, Addy?

MOMMA: *(smiling)* You look real nice, Sarah.

SARAH: *(proudly)* This my Christmas dress from last year.

ADDY: Do the girls dress real fancy at school?

SARAH: Some do. But don't you worry. *(She crosses the room to Addy.)* You look fine, Addy. You gonna like school. You'll see. *(She takes Addy's hand.)*

ADDY: Wish I could read.

SARAH: Not reading is nothing to be 'shamed about. Our teacher, Miss Dunn, will teach you to read. She taught me. And I can help you learn, too.

ADDY: I'd like that.

SARAH: I'm gonna help you, I promise.

MOMMA: *(handing a lunch pail to Addy)* Y'all be careful now. Go straight to school and come straight home after.

SARAH: *(hooking her arm in Addy's)* Don't worry, Mrs. Walker. I'm gonna look after Addy. I ain't gonna let nothing bad happen to her.

*(**Addy** and **Sarah** EXIT.)*

ACT TWO

Scene: The same morning, in the classroom. Addy and Sarah are seated together at a desk. Harriet sits at a desk in front of them.

*(**Miss Dunn** ENTERS. She stops next to Sarah.)*

MISS DUNN: Welcome back, Sarah. And who is your friend?

SARAH: This here is Addy Walker. She ain't never been to school before.

MISS DUNN: *(smiling in welcome)* I'm so pleased you're here, Addy. You may feel a bit confused this first week, but we'll help you learn your way.

ADDY: Thank you, ma'am.

*(**Miss Dunn** goes to the front of the classroom.)*

MISS DUNN: Good morning, boys and girls.
    I am Miss Dunn. I want you children who
    have been here before to help the new
    students. We'll begin our first day by
    copying the alphabet from the board.
    Sarah, please help Addy.

SARAH: Yes, ma'am. Look, Addy. *(demonstrating
    with the pencil)* Here's how you hold your
    pencil. And here's how you make the letters.
    (She pushes the slate and pencil over to Addy.)
    You try now.

*(**Addy** picks up the pencil, but it slips. She wraps her
whole hand around it and struggles to make the letters
as **Sarah** watches patiently and instructs her gently.)*

ADDY: My letters look squiggly and rough.

SARAH: *(encouraging)* Keep trying. *(She pauses
    as she watches Addy.)* Don't push down so
    hard. That's it. You doing fine.

(*Miss Dunn* approaches their desk and gently takes the slate pencil from Addy.)

MISS DUNN: (*writes on Addy's slate*) This is your name, Addy. I want you to practice it.

(*Miss Dunn* gives the slate pencil back to Addy, then moves on toward the front of the room.)

(*Addy* stares at the slate. *Sarah* nudges her.)

SARAH: Addy, you're s'posed to practice writing that.

ADDY: I know. It's just…this the first time I ever saw my name wrote down.

(*Addy* writes her name, looks dissatisfied, erases it, and writes it again very slowly. *Sarah* looks at it.)

SARAH: That's good, Addy. I can read that plain as day. (*spelling it out loud*) A-D-D-Y. You're good at learning.

ADDY: You're good at teaching.

(The two friends smile at each other.)

MISS DUNN: And now, boys and girls, I will
assign permanent desk partners. Addy,
you'll share a desk with Harriet.

SARAH: Miss Dunn, can Addy stay with me?
I been helping her.

MISS DUNN: No, Sarah. I want Addy to sit near
the front of the room.

*(**Addy** stands up and walks to the front of the room.
She smiles shyly as she sits next to Harriet. **Harriet**
doesn't smile back.)*

HARRIET: Do you know the alphabet?

ADDY: I'm just learning it. Sarah was teaching
me.

HARRIET: Sarah? Humph! *(in a snotty voice)* Sarah can hardly read herself! *I'll* help you. Miss Dunn put you with me because I'm the smartest one in the class.

ADDY: Sarah smart, too.

HARRIET: *(shakes her head in disagreement)* I'm named after Harriet Tubman. She helped run the Underground Railroad. You probably didn't know that. I know plenty of things like that. Now that Miss Dunn put you with me, I can teach you things. I might even invite you to study with me at my house.

ADDY: I bet your house is pretty.

HARRIET: Of course.

MISS DUNN: Boys and girls, it's time for lunch now.

*(**Harriet** rises quickly and EXITS with **Miss Dunn**.)*

*(**Sarah** gets out of her desk and crosses to Addy, who is still seated.)*

SARAH: How you like sitting with Harriet?

ADDY: She real smart and she got fine clothes. I wish I had a dress as pretty as the one she has on.

SARAH: Humph!

ADDY: What's the matter? Don't you like Harriet?

SARAH: That ain't it. Harriet don't like *me*. She all full of herself. She think she better than other people. If your family ain't got no money, she don't like you. And you know my family's poor.

ADDY: But Harriet was nice to me, and she know my family's poor.

SARAH: *(sincerely)* Listen, Addy. She was only nice 'cause Miss Dunn told her to be. Harriet don't have no poor girls like us for her friends. She gonna try to make you her slave. She tried it with me when I came to school last year, but I wouldn't let her. That's why she don't like me. She gonna hurt you just like she hurt me last year.

ADDY: *(hopefully)* Well, maybe Harriet changed from when you first come up here. Harriet ain't gonna hurt me. She say she got plenty to teach me, and I got plenty to learn.

*(**Harriet** ENTERS.)*

HARRIET: Addy, are you coming to lunch?

ADDY: Yes! Come on, Sarah.

SARAH: *(softly)* I ain't going with her.

HARRIET: *(in a snotty voice)* I heard you, Sarah. Nobody asked you to come. *(She turns away from Sarah.)* But you can come if you want, Addy. Sarah isn't the boss of you. It's your decision.

> *(**Harriet** EXITS. **Addy** watches her go but does not follow her.)*

ACT THREE

Scene: Outside Mrs. Ford's dress shop, after school, about three weeks later.

*(**Sarah** and **Addy** ENTER, stage right, carrying lunch pails. **Sarah** carries a bunch of grapes, which the girls are sharing. The door to Mrs. Ford's dress shop is stage left. The girls talk and eat grapes as they walk slowly across the stage to the shop. They stop walking when they reach the door of the shop.)*

ADDY: *(worried)* Miss Dunn say we gonna have a spelling match in two weeks. I'm gonna have to spell better than I do now or I'll be put out in the first round of the match.

SARAH: But you only been in school three weeks now.

ADDY: But it seems like I ain't never gonna catch up. Younger girls can read and spell better than me. Maybe it's too late for me to learn.

SARAH: *(kindly)* It ain't never too late. You can't learn everything at once. Learning go slow. I didn't do so good on yesterday's spelling test, neither. I should've studied harder.

ADDY: *(frustrated)* I studied hard and I *still* didn't do good. *(stopping to face Sarah)* How many did you get right?

(Sarah stops, too, and the girls face each other as they talk and share the grapes.)

SARAH: How many did *you* get right?

ADDY: I asked first.

SARAH: Well, I got all twenty wrong 'cause
I didn't study at all. *(sadly)* My poppa can't
hardly find work, so my momma and me
been taking in extra washing. Sometimes
I ain't got time to do my lessons.

ADDY: I got twelve wrong. *(shaking her head)*
You and me ain't like Harriet. You should
see her papers. All 100s. She already doing
multiplication. Schoolwork come easy to
her. I bet she'll win the spelling match
without hardly studying. And did you see
that blue dress she had on yesterday? It
was so pretty. I never even seen it before.
She must have ten or fifteen dresses. *(She
eats the last grape.)*

SARAH: *(annoyed)* Let's talk about something
else. *(starting to walk again)* I don't like
talking about Harriet, or even thinking
about her.

ADDY: I do. Harriet has everything I dreamed freedom would bring me. She got fancy dresses. She smart. She sure of herself.

SARAH: *(sarcastically)* She sure is.

ADDY: Harriet say she gonna invite me to her house so we can study spelling together.

SARAH: *(matter-of-factly)* But she ain't invited you yet.

ADDY: No, not yet. I can't wait to see her house.

SARAH: *(firmly)* Addy, I done warned you about Harriet. She ain't…

*(Sarah is interrupted when **Momma** ENTERS, coming out of the door of the shop. She is carrying packages and crying.)*

ADDY: Momma, what's the matter?

MOMMA: *(wiping her eyes and blowing her nose)* I'm supposed to deliver these packages for Mrs. Ford. But I can't read the addresses, so I don't know where to go.

ADDY: *(taking the packages)* Sarah and I can deliver them, Momma. Sarah can read way better than me, and she know her way around Philadelphia.

SARAH: *(looking at the addresses on the packages)* I know where these streets is!

MOMMA: *(drying her eyes)* I guess I ain't got a right to this job because I ain't been honest about not reading. I gotta learn to read or find something else to do.

ADDY: *(touches Momma's arm)* Momma, I can teach you how to read. And I'll get practice from helping you.

MOMMA: I think it's too late for me to learn.

ADDY: *(enthusiastically)* Sarah say it ain't never too late.

SARAH: *(nods her head)* That's right!

MOMMA: *(hugs Sarah)* You a big help, Sarah. I don't know what we'd do without you.

ADDY: We'll have our first lesson tonight, Momma.

MOMMA: *(Smiling, she hugs Addy.)* All right, Addy. I'll try. Ain't no change coming overnight, but by and by maybe we'll both learn.

ADDY: We will, Momma. You'll see!

*(**Addy** and **Sarah** EXIT with the packages.)*

ACT FOUR

Scene: Outside Mrs. Ford's dress shop, after school, two weeks later.

*(**Addy** and **Sarah** ENTER, carrying lunch pails and books. They stop when **Addy** bends down to tie her boot lace.)*

SARAH: You ready for the spelling match tomorrow?

ADDY: I hope so. I been studying every night.

*(**Harriet** and **Mavis** ENTER, carrying books and lunch pails. **Addy** picks up her lunch pail and books and stands up again.)*

HARRIET: *(ignoring Sarah)* Well, Addy, are you going to walk home with Mavis and me today, or do you have to ask Sarah's permission?

ADDY: I don't have to ask her permission. *(excitedly)* I'm gonna walk with you.

HARRIET: *(smugly)* Good.

ADDY: *(turns to smile at Sarah)* Sarah, you can come, too.

SARAH: No, I can't. You go on. You know you want to. *(She blinks hard to fight back tears.)* I don't care.

*(**Sarah** turns away and EXITS.)*

*(**Addy** watches Sarah leave. **Harriet** and **Mavis** pile their books on top of Addy's.)*

ADDY: These are kinda heavy. Why I got to carry them all?

HARRIET: *(firmly)* You're the new girl. You have to do what we say.

MAVIS: That's right.

*(**Harriet** and **Mavis** look at each other and giggle. Then, as they all begin to walk along, **Harriet** takes an apple out of her pocket or her lunch pail.)*

HARRIET: Did you see Sarah's dress today? It was so wrinkled, it looked like she slept in it. *(She throws the apple in the air once or twice, then tosses it to Mavis.)*

MAVIS: *(dropping behind Addy to catch the apple)* And it had a big brown stain on the front.

ADDY: *(struggling not to drop all the books as she watches them toss the apple)* That don't matter.

HARRIET: *(catching the apple again)* Of course it matters. Anyway, what do you care about Sarah? You're on our side now. At least *you* look presentable.

*(By this time the girls are in front of the door to Mrs. Ford's dress shop, where they stop. **Harriet** and **Mavis** exchange a look. They take their books back. **Harriet** takes a bite of the apple.)*

MAVIS: This is where you live, isn't it, Addy?

ADDY: Yes, but I thought I was going home with y'all today. Momma said I can study at your house, Harriet.

HARRIET: I don't think so. Not today.

ADDY: *(protesting)* But the spelling match is tomorrow. You promised…

HARRIET: *(firmly)* Not today. Come on, Mavis.

*(**Harriet** and **Mavis** EXIT, hurrying away. Addy is left alone, looking very sad.)*

ACT FIVE

Scene: In the classroom, the next morning. Addy, Harriet, and Sarah stand in a line facing Miss Dunn for the spelling match.

MISS DUNN: Harriet, spell "carriage."

HARRIET: *(spelling quickly)* C-A-R-R-I-A-G-E.

MISS DUNN: Sarah, you have the next word. Spell "button."

SARAH: *(slowly and carefully)* B-U-T-T-O-N.

MISS DUNN: Addy, it's your turn. Spell "tomorrow."

ADDY: T-O-M-O-R-O *(She stops and starts again.)* T-O-M-O-R-R-O-W.

MISS DUNN: Correct.

HARRIET: *(whispers to Addy)* I'm going to win, and my mother said I can have friends over after school for ice cream to celebrate. I might ask you.

*(**Addy** smiles.)*

*(**Sarah** looks at Addy and Harriet and turns away unhappily.)*

MISS DUNN: Harriet, spell "doctor."

HARRIET: *(quickly)* D-O-C-T-O-R.

MISS DUNN: Sarah, spell "account."

SARAH: A-C-C- *(She stops and starts again, unsure.)* A-C-C-O-N-T.

MISS DUNN: I'm sorry. That's not correct.

*(**Sarah** sits down, looking disappointed.)*

HARRIET: *(whispers to Addy)* I can't believe Sarah missed such an easy one. She is so dumb.

MISS DUNN: Addy, now you must spell "account."

ADDY: A-C-C-O-U-N-T.

MISS DUNN: Good, Addy. Harriet, only you and Addy are left. Spell "principle." We all live our lives by *principles*. "Principle."

HARRIET: P-R-I-N-S-I-P-L-E.

MISS DUNN: I'm sorry. That is not correct. Addy, you must spell the word correctly to win. "Principle."

ADDY: P-R-I-N-<u>C</u>-I-P-L-E.

MISS DUNN: *(delightedly)* Correct! Addy Walker, you have truly earned this prize. Your hard work has paid off.

*(**Miss Dunn** pins a medal on Addy, who beams with pride.)*

MISS DUNN: Congratulations, Addy. And now, you are all excused for lunch. *(She turns to erase the chalkboard.)*

HARRIET: *(smugly)* Well, if I had studied at all, I would have beaten you. Anyway, Miss Dunn gave you easier words. *(She crosses to the door and looks back at Addy.)* I'm eating lunch out on the front steps if you want to join me and my friends.

*(Hearing what Harriet has said, **Sarah** puts her head down on her desk.)*

*(**Harriet** EXITS, flouncing out.)*

MISS DUNN: *(crosses to Addy and puts her hands on Addy's shoulders)* This is a very special day for you, Addy. But you don't look very happy.

ADDY: *(sadly)* Miss Dunn, I done hurt Sarah, and I wouldn't blame her if she never spoke to me again.

MISS DUNN: *(looks over at Sarah, whose head is still down)* But I am sure she would *listen* to you. Why don't you go talk to her and tell her how you feel?

*(**Miss Dunn** EXITS.)*

*(**Addy** thinks for a few seconds, then goes to her desk to look inside her lunch pail. She carries it back to Sarah's desk.)*

ADDY: *(sitting next to Sarah, who looks up)* I'm so sorry, Sarah. Please forgive me. I wanted to be friends with Harriet because she's popular and smart and rich. But she ain't a real friend. *(pauses)* I know you is. I never meant to hurt you. *(holds out her hand)* I want you to still be my friend.

SARAH: *(taking Addy's hand)* I still want to be your friend. *(pauses, then smiles)* And I wanted you to win the spelling match so bad.

ADDY: I wanted you to win, too. I was sad when you missed your word. Maybe we can study spelling together right now. *(She reaches into her lunch pail and smiles as she pulls something out of it. She holds out four cookies on her outstretched hand, each in the shape of a letter.)* Look, Sarah. Momma made me cookies in the shapes of the letters I'm teaching her. Here's our first word!

*(As **Addy** hands the cookies one at a time to Sarah, they spell the letters out loud together.)*

ADDY and **SARAH:** L-O-V-E.

ADDY: *(smiling)* Love's the best word to start with.

TIPS FOR ACTORS

🌟 Use your imagination. If you don't have a fancy stage or elaborate props and costumes, act as if you do!

🌟 Speak clearly and loudly enough to be heard. Don't turn your back to the audience or stand between another actor and the audience.

🌟 Pretend that you **are** the character you are playing. If you forget your lines and can't hear the prompter, think about what the character would really say and say it in your own words.

🌟 Act and speak at the same time. Directions before your lines will tell you things to do as you are saying those lines. For example,

> (**Miss Dunn** *pins a medal on Addy.*)
>
> **MISS DUNN:** Congratulations, Addy.

🌟 Other directions make suggestions about how to say a line. For example,

> **SARAH:** *(proudly)* This my Christmas dress from last year.

🌟 Cooperate with the director and the other actors. And don't forget to smile at the curtain call!